A Note to Parents and Caregivers:

Read-it! Joke Books are for children who are moving ahead on the amazing road to reading. These fun books support the acquisition and extension of reading skills as well as a love of books.

Published by the same company that produces *Read-it!* Readers, these books introduce the question/answer and dialogue patterns that help children expand their thinking about language structure and book formats.

When sharing joke books with a child, read in short stretches. Pause often to talk about the meaning of the jokes. The question/answer and dialogue formats work well for this purpose and provide an opportunity to talk about the language and meaning of the jokes. Have the child turn the pages and point to the pictures and familiar words. When you read the jokes, have fun creating the voices of characters or emphasizing some important words. Be sure to reread favorite jokes.

There is no right or wrong way to share books with children. Find time to read with your child, and pass on the legacy of literacy.

Adria F. Klein, Ph.D.
Professor Emeritus
California State University
San Bernardino, California

Editor: Jill Kalz
Designer: Joe Anderson
Page Production: Melissa Kes
Creative Director: Keith Griffin
Editorial Director: Carol Jones
The illustrations in this book were created digitally.

Picture Window Books
5115 Excelsior Boulevard
Suite 232
Minneapolis, MN 55416
877-845-8392
www.picturewindowbooks.com

Printed in the United States of America.

Library of Congress Cataloging-in-Publication Data
Donahue, Jill L.
Silly sports : a book of sports jokes / by Jill L. Donahue ; illustrated by Amy Bailey
Muehlenhardt.
p. cm. — (Read-it! joke books—supercharged!)
Includes bibliographical references.
ISBN-13: 978-1-4048-2366-2 (hardcover)
ISBN-10: 1-4048-2366-2 (hardcover)
1. Sports—Juvenile humor. 2. Riddles, Juvenile. I. Muehlenhardt, Amy Bailey, 1974–
II. Title. III. Series.
PN6231.S65D66 2007
818'.602—dc22   2006003406

Silly Sports

A Book of Sports Jokes

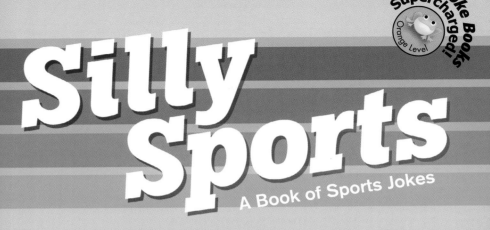

by Jill L. Donahue
illustrated by Amy Bailey Muehlenhardt

Special thanks to our advisers for their expertise:

Adria F. Klein, Ph.D.
Professor Emeritus, California State University
San Bernardino, California

Susan Kesselring, M.A.
Literacy Educator
Rosemount–Apple Valley–Eagan (Minnesota) School District

In baseball, why does it take longer to run from second base to third base than it does to run from first base to second base?
Because there is a shortstop between second base and third base.

Why was Cinderella bad at basketball?
She had a pumpkin for a coach.

Which football players can jump higher than the goalpost?

All of them—goalposts can't jump!

Why shouldn't you tell a joke when you are ice-skating?

The ice might crack up.

Why did the lawyer pack a tennis racquet in his briefcase?

He was going to court.

How do fireflies start a race?

Someone shouts, "Ready ... set ... glow!"

What color are cheerleaders?
YELLow.

Why did the coach go to the bank?
He wanted his quarterback.

Why did the volleyball coach want the waitress to join his team?
He heard she was a good server.

Why can't you go fishing if your watch is broken?

You won't have the time.

Why did the softball player have to go to jail?

She got caught stealing third base.

What is a runner's favorite subject?

Jography.

In what part of a ballpark do you find the whitest clothes?

In the bleachers.

What team cries when it loses?
A "ball" club.

Why is baseball the richest sport?
Because baseball fields have large diamonds.

Why does the air feel hot after a softball game?
Because all of the fans leave.

Why did the ocean take the afternoon off?
It wanted to play "gulf" for a while.

What did the basketball player wear to her school dance?
A hoop skirt.

What are the best kinds of stockings for baseball players to wear?

Stockings with runs in them.

How is a scrambled egg like a losing team?

They both are beaten.

What kinds of cats like to go bowling?

Alley cats.

Where do catchers, batters, and pitchers dance?
At the Base Ball.

How is a crate of peaches like a car racetrack?
They both have pits.

Boy: "Hey, Dad! I was responsible for the winning run in today's baseball game!"

Dad: "That's great! How did you do that?"

Boy: "I dropped the ball, and the runner went right past me to score the run."

Why was night baseball started?

Because bats like to sleep in the daytime.

What is the best way to win a race?

Run faster than everybody else!

What did the basketball say to the basketball player?

"You've really got me going through hoops for you."

What is the best advice to give a young baseball player?

"If you don't succeed at first, try second base."

Why did the basketball player cancel his airline ticket?

He didn't want to get caught traveling.

Why did the golfer bring a cage to the golf course?

She was hoping to get some birdies.

Why did the exterminator hire a bunch of outfielders?

He needed people who were good at catching flies.

What is a referee from Italy called?

A Roman umpire.

What is the biggest team of all?
The New York Giants.

What kind of drink do football players avoid?
Penalty.

How are swimming pools, bowling alleys, and store check-out areas all the same?
They all have lanes.

Why did the wrestler bring his mom's sewing kit to the match?

He wanted to pin his opponent.

Why did the golfer wear his socks without any shoes?

He was hoping to get a hole in one.

What is the difference between a boxer and a man with a cold?

One knows his blows, and the other blows his nose.

What do a dog and a baseball player have in common?

They both chase strays and run for home when they see the catcher.

Why does every soccer team need a ghost?

To be their ghoulkeeper.

What did the gymnast say to the mat?

"I'm head over heels for you."

What has 18 legs and catches flies?

A baseball team.

When the two balls of string raced each other, who won?
Neither. They were tied.

How are pancakes and baseball alike?
They both depend on the batter.

What kinds of stories do basketball players tell?

Tall tales.

What kinds of stories do anglers tell?

Fish tales.

Read-it! Joke Books— Supercharged!

Looking for a specific title or level? A complete list
of *Read-it!* Readers is available on our Web site:
www.picturewindowbooks.com